Scared Text

THE COLORADO PRIZE FOR POETRY

Strike Anywhere, by Dean Young
selected by Charles Simic, 1995

Summer Mystagogia, by Bruce Beasley
selected by Charles Wright, 1996

The Thicket Daybreak, by Catherine Webster
selected by Jane Miller, 1997

Palma Cathedral, by Michael White
selected by Mark Strand, 1998

Popular Music, by Stephen Burt
selected by Jorie Graham, 1999

Design, by Sally Keith
selected by Allen Grossman, 2000

A Summer Evening, by Geoffrey Nutter
selected by Jorie Graham, 2001

Chemical Wedding, by Robyn Ewing
selected by Fanny Howe, 2002

Goldbeater's Skin, by G. C. Waldrep
selected by Donald Revell, 2003

Whethering, by Rusty Morrison
selected by Forrest Gander, 2004

Frayed escort, by Karen Garthe
selected by Cal Bedient, 2005

Carrier Wave, by Jaswinder Bolina
selected by Lyn Hejinian, 2006

Brenda Is in the Room and Other Poems,
by Craig Morgan Teicher
selected by Paul Hoover, 2007

One Sun Storm, by Endi Bogue Hartigan
selected by Martha Ronk, 2008

The Lesser Fields, by Rob Schlegel
selected by James Longenbach, 2009

Annulments, by Zach Savich
selected by Donald Revell, 2010

Scared Text, by Eric Baus
selected by Cole Swensen, 2011

Scared Text

ERIC BAUS

The Center for Literary Publishing
COLORADO STATE UNIVERSITY

For information about permission to reproduce
selections from this book, write to
Permissions, Center for Literary Publishing,
9105 Campus Delivery, Department of English,
Colorado State University,
Fort Collins, Colorado 80523-9105.

Printed in the United States of America.

Library of Congress Cataloging-in-Publication Data
Baus, Eric.
  Scared text / Eric Baus.
      p. cm. -- (The Colorado Prize for Poetry)
ISBN 978-1-885635-18-1 (pbk. : alk. paper) --
ISBN 978-1-885635-24-2 (electronic)
  I. Title.
  PS3602.A97S33 2011
  811'.6--dc23
  2011037732

The paper used in this book meets the minimum requirements of the
American National Standard for Information Sciences-Permanence of
Paper for Printed Library Materials, ANSI Z39.48-1984.

1 2 3 4 5   15 14 13 12 11

for Andrea Rexilius

Contents

NEGATIVE NOON

Stupid Moon	25
Glass Deer	26
Gored Ox	27
Negative Noon	28
Urned Braid	32
An Ember	33

PUMA MIRAGE

Hornet Fleece	37
Puma Mirage	38
Coma Silt	39
Exoskeletal Gesture	41
Clovered Ohms	42

FLOODED CLOUD

Minotaur Stable

GLASS EAR

Approach the smallest ghost after he has turned his back. A buzz of definition surrounds him. This is the sting of the fleeing beetle. How soon before the house becomes soot? The statue of elderly hornets is delicately connected to the floor. On the other side of the wall an apple hangs suspended. There is no such thing as "There is no ghost."

ATTIC GRASSES

A ghost's frost blooms inside a glass vase. But what does the swarming sky do? Why has the sound of a boy disappeared? A not-body, not not beaming, resets. Becomes a bee revived with ether. Booming, ten beetle stings make the bottle break. This is a picture of a boy without a mouse. Being animal in the attic grasses.

SPOILED SWAN

A clod of spoiled swan applied to his twin fails to infuse the ground with glands. The elated bells in his brain have grown knotted. Even the most active worms refuse to gloss the sod. Has the sun repaired yet? How to solve for its abscess? Behind the bricks is a wall of false glass. Follow the trail to the minotaur stable. Be a diorama.

MIRROR SEED

The sky divided and so did I. I watched my mirror seed a cloud. The house rained. Identical heads echoed. A dead oud's resonance cloned the first presence. An apple in the attic developed a tree. I felt the sun.

I fell into an open field. The clone smiled. I have never seen a clone smile. His snails grew fur. The closest ant grafted the smoke with sand. This is the first piece of wood. This is the first piece of glass. Clouds arranged them behind dead doves. The membrane's séance broke. The doves died again. The dead doves reset. I arranged them into flowers. I have never seen a flower. I have never seen a dove.

The sky and its stills mated. I have never played an oud. I have never said Bird. *O snail,* I heard outside. When the first dove died, the ouds ate apples. I died too. My glass fermented opals. The second séance failed, my fur glued to flowers. I have never seen a cloud. I have never looked down. The organ smoked. The clone strummed. I fled, immersed in flames. The mirror chimed. Dove. Oud. Field. The bloomed membrane's array split. Inside, the blanks bred herds.

A DELPHI

Minus tried to write his own bible. It began, *So what, saliva. So what, milk.*

Iris told us her dad died in space. The whited-out vowels rang in my ears. *Stupid moon. Stupid burned-up blind spot.*

The doctors said his name had burned up. We never knew how it sounded.

✽

The city refused to see my brother. He banged out his nerves on birthdays. *I use years, and they remember.*

This was in the annex of the indivisible.

Escape your leaves, Minus said. I said, *I have never used camouflage.* It felt so good to lie, all that noise loosening inside me.

I like lies.

✽

The burned-up hills had grown more graceful.

I like hills.

They feel like hands.

*

When I wasn't looking Iris re-named her tongue. *Hey, Solo Swarm.*

Her questioning pulled. *Why are you always floating?*

She said she tried to sign my name but the ink was immature. *Stupid minutes.*

*

The city wasn't looking. This city wasn't old enough to look.

The city said, *This city isn't old enough to say.*

*

Minus told me not to breathe when the doctors floated by. He sat on the floor and covered his mouth. I hid behind the blinds.

This was in the entrance of the opposite pharmacy.

Minus's bible began to speak. *Hey, Solo Swarm,* it streamed. Iris's saliva was turning sharp, straining itself through her teeth.

*

In the organs of her father's owl, Iris heard half of her name.

My brother threw a brick at its head. He was helping his cells divide.

Iris scratched the city's face with the keys she had in her hand.

Whatever the opposite of prophecy was was what I was listening for.

*

The city decided to follow me home. *Can I ask you a question?* it said.

I put my gum in the subway slot to keep it from saying my name.

Hey, Owl Boy, can you hear me? Hey, Mister Face, what's your name?

I would like to be called A DIFFERENT HOUSE. I would like to be oxen and bread.

*

Minus water. Minus air. Inside the house with a tree growing through it.

I woke up alone with my feet in the branches. I woke up behind the sky.

The doctors took the needles out without removing my sheet.

Iris was outside holding her breath. My brother had floated away.

*

The city appointed a second owl to see if my brother had drowned.

The owl was sifting the blanks in our herd. The city was clovered in sound.

I like noise.

Iris likes space. She thinks it feels like snow.

*

My brother returned from the burned-up hills. He contracted a diffident voice.

Whenever I asked him a question he branched. He woke up outside his breath.

☆

Minus's bible was reading itself. All those invisible vowels.

Crossing out the sky, the landscape stretched, moving the apex of the so-called.

An inverse tone accrued in my tongue. The octave's egress bruised.

☆

Iris awoke with wool in her mouth. Grass grew over her eyes.

The doctors thought she had seen the bad wheat. *She will need a second reading.*

Minus's blindness spread to his hands. His fingers were starting to slow.

☆

Inscribed, blighted, tongue filled with snow. A throat so other I entered my name.

The blotted-out passages hummed. *Beetles bloomed underfoot.*

This was in the attic of a different house.

I slept throughout the stings.

Molting Solos

THE UR-MANE

In classical buried-birth narratives, the immersed egg frequently feels both mammoth and absent, sedated with seeds. It says, *A cataclysmic dial is upon us.*

THE WORM'S FIRST FILM

Two horses climb a hive. The plumage around their waists retracts. *I ate mace,* one thinks. *No one knows I ate mace.* His mouth repeats a top lip twice. *Don't tell my brother. Please.*

A still shows his core is a molting eel. It ekes some light then glows back in its hole. It grows glass from its face. It sleets.

No blinking, he says to himself, through his peel. He blinds his own ivory with the finest lamps. Does he seed a dot of blood? Do his teeth feed leaves? Clouds polish him plush. This is the last fence, dust.

VOTIVE SCORES

If eels lie vertically inside the statue or old bees coat its surface, a needle will point to the center of my hide. Owls murmured up a piece of green cloth. Hard ash topped me. The birds it entailed peopled the treetops, stripped me of my coos. Un-tuned doves flew elsewhere, worried their drones would shrink inside my ears. A second split occurred when its eyes bloomed red. Votive scores pushed open the view. Here, the street was both omen and throat. The swarming sky sparrowed until day withered, until the statue punched out of its skin. He was wearing his own arms. His house showed. Ants formed and he scorched their trails. *Sing rendered.* he trilled, *Sing posed.*

CANARY ARIA

When a canary's aria dredged the fringe from a drowned colt, it inherited its way of breaking apart. Differing is one long moment. We cannot divide its songs.

MOLTING SOLOS

The first pair of giraffes is the most metallic, but the captive asp in the center of the nest alternates between solid and signified knives. One grew blurred, and must be resisted. Look at it. Look at its tongue. Imagine the back of the thought that it crosses. Why was it so difficult to picture a bird?

*

The intensity of elephants should continue beyond the title and merge back into the figure of mud. This lion is, therefore, like the lion following a marionette. Here, their passage is called brothering moss, and elsewhere, the hand that distinguishes between rains. Each finger implies another flame.

*

Although there was a bird chirping, the emphasis was still on the ground. New likenesses assemble an absence, an audience of dissident listening, each of their faces quoted, quilted, singing A SOLO FOR SWARMS. The empty sleeves their ears become wander, rehearsing inside of a herd.

CLONE BURNS

A cod ate itself. A cod ate itself and in eating itself dons a clone. The clone burns. The burning clouds. The cod's cloud burst into throngs.

EGGSHELL PLUMBS

Blurted, The Ur-Mane erupts, combs through growls to the coarsest salt. A thimble full of eggshell plumbs the egresses for slits. I listen for the second salt, to two horns: locked, alloyed. A moan inverts an ant, burns out in bursts. Its lisps form pools, stinging ice, clips of aberrant grass. See how green I can be. So stirred. A stem empties a range of sheep. A still invents its scene. I plead with all the strays to heap. A shark in a mason jar, scared. Such smooth. So screen. I cut to a tree.

Negative Noon

STUPID MOON

Whatever poisoned wave stands to block its beginning. Whether torn dove or stunned moth. In the bind. In the polished blank of a sun. How faded our horse is, starts.

GLASS DEER

Here is how to hand a glass deer a beetle. Here is how to bind the bloom over its mouth. The sun a moth is in a strong clot of ether blinds its antlers. It hollows its ears. Inside is the song a twinned flute splits. A silent gong. An elongated stitch.

GORED OX

A man with a lantern buried the tail of a gored ox in reddened wool. Both sands said this. Minus inscribed, *Bathed in salt, a new bus arrives.* A cold fit. Should wood be laced into the scene as ash? Embers hot, he saw another fold of the vellum effect. Would his story sleet? Was the elemental udder set to speech? A flayed colt, Iris interred the oration of a thorn. She saw inside the funerary soot. He was tainted to depict the birth of a thrush. He was an only arson, an anvil inside. Iris was cited in cloud position, as Ibis. Ibis, twice the size of a flock. An enemy of ices, her urn became a fish. Had Ibis's urn contained a clone? The story striated, swallowed an asp.

NEGATIVE NOON

Oxen are bad.

Oxen are bad? Minus adjusted the clone's hand. The hand grew cold. I heard his oud die. Dead, bad oxen.

His shoulder creak caused a sting in my ear. His modes merged, formed a team. *Aphid wounds make the house hurt,* he said.

My gut needs cake. The seared core tugged. I spoke my title and he hissed: *Do not impinge upon my robes. No tent goes untorn.*

More glint, these beasts are ill. An abbreviation for beaten.

✻

More gongs, enough to tear the room apart. Minus decoded "f" with theater pins. Divorced the curved curves chords have.

How would Iris play the hollowed-out end of an ark rack? we hounded. Iris wandered out, assaulted by doves. Teal caskets.

"f" is a forlorn purr. It beguiles dull sentries. The rooms in the fort fit together in a series of steel forgeries. Vials emit a mist of yes. If the clang from the hall revolver dies, hordes unite inside tombs.

His snores blow out lamps. Lest his lungs grow hot.

✼

These nests end. These nests end, he blurred in his sleep. The cobra button broke loose until his cell glowed negative noon.

Winding the loom like an idiot ant, I tried to reverse the topiary trap.

Day hissed and our teeth tuned in. Our dirty arms got sunny. Quills dragged tongs across our names. I died to walk away. My dead doves reddened. Their puma leered while the coos waned.

Medicine stored in their breath became bulbous. Was cud coalescing?

The story stormed. The shorn grew gills.

✼

Only Minus's halo remained. Can helium herd? Could aluminum clot? Beastlessness disturbed the din. *O corn,* we cried instead.

Doubled eels loomed, but what I fished for was a hiss that talked backwards.

Deep in the inert clouds, an analogy splits. A cold sardine awakens. Amber anemones flower shards.

*

Is this the ember's big splice? we clanged, as the city's signal burned.

Iris's multiples flung about, wed to interference. *Hover longer, eater of bells, every angle ignites a wing.*

Mirrored wheat. Thuds.

To deter owls, we use the azure comb. *I am tired,* says Iris, *and the ants are staring.* Minus plumbs an urn large enough for all the sentinel's prayers. Ten surly lions.

*

This is Minus's House. Bombs infuse blooms here.

When Minus isn't posturing, Iris is queen of the gray distance. Pre-gray, free. As in, *Hand me another dosed star.* As in, *Sing rendered. Sing posed.*

*

Act terminated.

The blood oasis lengthens in the leaves outside. The tomb sends its allies home. Minus and Iris paint over the bones.

When the datura plains revert to "f" Iris instructs her brother to sing "f" but the "f shield" in the ghost's hand lures owls instead.

Minus knots nicely in the fire. Our allies await.

*

My system slowed down to place a pleat in the fountain. Nobody moots my calm.

Beasts booed while cranes ate smashed apples.

Minus entered a pensive shadow. Clear molds dented Iris's brain. The tiniest cloud put a plume in my hair.

The imperfect thread of our clinging hands will never blend its theses.

When the opposite scale begins to beehive, we'll feel the hair of The Ur-Mane.

URNED BRAID

If Minus writhes after a séance, mostly cloud, out in the unscreened air, bees comb his hair. Night heat made his ink weave neon. His cells grew a negative moon. Did serum sprawl during the previous incubation of The Ur-Mane? Honed nils emerged. An orange fur. Born back to beetle gel, he slit the coma's hide.

AN EMBER

When Iris was asleep, she was seeing salt, seeing what salt says it is. She was trying to explain "sistence." There was a sifter beside her. *An ember,* she said. Her reading was a foam reddening, a painting over a page. A film of her tongue, an orange film. A pool to watch while the ground arrived.

Puma Mirage

HORNET FLEECE

Two foxes inject the weather with stilts. They fuse to be parsed from their bleating. They seed. There are several kings in a single fox. They haunt one another's brows. They hunt their brains for a broken stinger. A crown of hornets fleeces their phlox.

PUMA MIRAGE

The Ur-Mane invented a puma mirage. Its ears rang inside its own ears. Stupid purrs. The puma's image lapsed as it foraged for footprints. The silhouette grew large and it spilled. The puma's shadow absorbed a horse. It was called The Blur when it stirred.

COMA SILT

Inside Minus's sleeping skull, a clamor diffused an imploded coda.

He heard it through a bruised channel. Voices wrapped in glass.

✻

Iris's blinks sedated her story. Molting solos, her shards wreathed the sea.

A follower of eels, she steeped herself in ether. Beetle tincture qualmed her hair.

✻

Abscessed opals in Minus's eyes glossed the ground for waves.

Swallowed thorns recorded the travel of a frozen phoneme's tail.

✻

Iris decoded the primal sting from a pile of puréed bees.

Their pollen perfumed her tongue with a tomb. Its flowers bloomed sour, interred.

✻

Minus's ivory cried in his teeth while the oxen's entrails quarreled.

Their marks were made in remaindered sugar. Their hay was a halo of wasps.

✻

Beyond a patch of occluded pumas, Iris immersed in the river's dredge.

The Blur exhumed its beams as a siren. It minted a signal in weeds.

✻

Iris reprised Minus's brain with fumes from a pulverized king.

This was the film that forgot how to mirror. The heap scanned as AMBULANCE SCENE.

✻

Minus's sanctuary had burst. His floor was an acre of snakes.

The most merged lion circled outside. A ghost coterminous with the lantern's demise.

40

EXOSKELETAL GESTURE

Venom erupted from the trees when the vital system of the brook reset its serum stem. Can suspended snakes compose a more careless music? Do two detached wings count as an exoskeletal gesture? A hiss is the sound the sky would make if these leaves revived their flight.

CLOVERED OHMS

Minus fled the river when the current sprouted dust. I walked in circles so
the powdered clouds would pass. Iris called back, pronounced herself out.
Walked back to her feet. Amended. As if she'd been cured in a salty brook.
As if eggshells glossed the inverse of her skin: *For the migratory door, there is no
such thing as East.* Clovered ohms accrued in her place.

Ox Tongue

DOVE BOMB

The landscape hissed a reddened cloud. The birth of a blurted scene.
Immersed in dead nets, the sky appointed a burned-up beast to calm the city's
tomb. The ox cried, stunned to see a crowd that had drowned in the dawn.
Fermented flowers amended its saliva. Doves burst beneath its tongue.

MIGRATORY DOOR

Another growl cancels the clouds. Some wind. Some flames. A swarm. Its exit opens a diorama. Here is the horse's pulse. Egrets watch a signal redden. The backs of their heads balloon. Surplus breath unearths a horn, a migratory door.

VARIANT AQUARIUM

The Ur-Mane egresses the variant aquarium. It is abstract, an illegible sea. A close-up of a close-up. This is the precursor of paralyzed film. The film cannot see itself until it becomes a creature, a terrified series of tiny black dots. Its head is me, the scariest version. I think, *I might include this in my larger animal. I know its movements.* This is the scene of a circular voice. *My eyes are a sequence of eyes,* it says.

LATENT VEINS

Iris severed her screens. It created the illusion of a latent vein. *I travel from speaker to singer,* she hovered, *across my elongated breadth. My river cannot swim. And I, the bodies it encounters, am found by a lion. It has a mechanical mane, but I force it to forget its story. I pause above its body. I forest it for water.*

✻

What Minus heard vented his head with strands of aberrant silk. The lament appended: *There is no boundary to being a lamb but there are brooks inside a wake.* He sealed his pupils in plumage. He fell to wet his tarps. The mollusk's membranes burst from him humming *I WOULD LIKE TO SIEVE MY SKIN.*

✻

My stills spilled. All I wanted was a meal of grass but my blood reversed its flight. I knelt. The marks on my chest implied a horse. It compelled me to pluck the black shark's harp. The Blur unfurled its fangs. It stung. I wept to sweep my surface for salt. The cursed hide covered our caskets with sand.

SPIRAL SCRAP

This is a cutting made from Iris. The spiral scrap on that slab of glass. Organs emit from the shavings of her story. The film in her muscles tears until two spilled waters sleet beside themselves. Her seam becomes a sibling of the frame this still is glossed from. The contours of her tendons guide her eyes through the shapes that entail the original look.

OX TONGUE

Minus's speech returned to worms. He smeared a gram of his lips on the ground. He tried to sing them A RUPTURE OF SOD but two ox tongues blocked that breath. Expelling the whorls alert in the grass, breezes re-sequenced his skin.

EGRET EYES

Iris's egret's eyes were filming I HAVE NEVER SEEN THE SUN. The scene begins with a vellum sea, then a field of the blurriest soot. A molting asp erodes a ghost's gowns until the corpse is absorbed. Posthumous clouds counsel the wind, and her pollen resigns from its home.

Scared Text

SCARED TEXT

Omnivores cannot survive. Which bus takes us to the submerged city? A vital, comprehensive explanation is essential for fauna. The malady intelligentsia has risen once again. More lava in the old auditorium is a blessing, the men said, because graceful calcium flows through us all.

It rained flames. Nested qualms sun themselves, whose somnolent mates will never solarize. No one can treat the corrupt sifter's core. In you, baroque valences convert. Stunted quills illuminate. Don latex, martyrs, the corporeal Yes pleads. Quartz purrs.

To the sandy cave, Amen. The buzzing of italics animates a quail. Home minus spirit. Erasers fail in various planes. The palace absorbs doctrine via sanctuary tomb. Its citizens merge amorphously. Does drama tame the face or is the forest sensing corpses? Whoever interrupts grace adds an animal to the fleet. Miss Minimum, an ex alto, delights our rusty ears with a solo, but the state requires a sextet for the committee of flame inquiry.

An alias for enemy, memory means the moan that precedes me. I am suspicious of the sun. Were hints neglected? Act posthumous. Neglect supplies us with a process. It adds No's to the primal sum. Our vigil ends in um, an upset.

Sickness spreads among the models. Tantrums. Axe horror. Desiccated parties roam. Bats suspend, turn violet, and enlarge. On the meditation bus, senators remain invisible. Should aluminum darts dissect squids? Indignant, fuming, the audience grows ill. Secular liquids infuse our spit. What is nobler, the medicinal figment or a vestige of errant sequins?

Horse discipline occupies the post-meridians. Verse deflects rats and mules in superstitious fables so precious, proper waters can enter the summit. One hundred lips hum with momentum, but when will the masked graves concur? Ink on the supreme participation tunic unearths a pelican trail. Clumped signs.

The animals in this village will have no dreams. A lasso prostration of the armada deduces none are more concrete than climate prophets. Only their formal digits may fumble the kiln's increased cavity for meals of gaudy deer. Curing non-beauty, the occupants' prayers present the name of the fortune umbrella. Torn monologues turn fluid in their litmus address.

Lamb Comb

OWL WOOL

The sky fermented a cotton tarp. The baffled voiceover spread. Iris's dove scored itself with scales while owl wool coated the cliffs.

DARK SUM

Sod apes itself and the potted horse becomes aloe. Sod apes a clotting O and clumps a dark sum. Mirages eat the magi. Their hum entombs a storm.

AQUA MANGE

Eel wool accrues in the osprey's tracks while the oil of drowned whales fills the spine of a swallow. If the eel's sarong ascends the surface, its coat refuses to plume. Like the weather in which each drone is immersed, the nests are resplendent with tusks. Sutured sea grass reverses to hide and the lions crash their combs.

PARALLEL PUMA

The Blur's recessive puma hatched a brother. Its cage was flowered with gills. Aphid burrs. The angles of the flora's surliest roaches eroded the circular gate. The house bayed. The spurned braids decoded. The puma's brother pounced to divide from its flight.

CREATURE'S CREATURE

The scopes Minus used to scan his silhouette developed latent veins in his eyes. He perceived a tail's erosion. *I am awake,* he said, *but I think I need to describe myself.* He tried to tell himself what a tongue was. It made a ball of ice, some smoke.

The mouth of the next thing he said came out clear. *I hid my hidden head. It starred.* He claimed it calmed his ghost whenever he spoke to the well of its engine.

He shook the snow from his clothes. No one whispered the destroyed elements that would have framed his silence. *Nothing,* he replied. *Nothing. I just told you my greatest secret.*

When he is sleeping in the riverbed, he lights up alluvial figures. Though not alone, he knows no more of the beings beyond him than to fear the sun. He recalled being posed. He thought, *I am being posed.*

And though he was perfectly fused from the sunlight, it was not exactly singing, what was seeding inside. As he turned his passages into their seasons, he let them be. He fished his shelves, then poured out the chimney.

A bundle of swollen strangers, he scared them, and all their trebles and springs retreated. He taught his beak to break the aviary open. He called himself Creature and Creature's Creature. It named the surface beneath his scales.

LAMB COMB

Iceless manger, endless ands, Iris cooed into their hooves. She perfumed the roof with silt. She played I HAVE SEEN THE LACE IN A PIN. Her hay was made of grass. It waved. It sifted all their tufts.

STUNNED COVE

Iris embered her story. *I was a sister wearing down.* She was etched in ash. She was sewn. She thought her mane would be sunned and it was. It was an Ibis on the banks, a mast.

Flooded Cloud

NEGATIVE MOON

Minus magnetized his story's satellites to form a negative moon. His echoes unearthed a hidden gong stored inside the core. The cloaked tone spread. Impacted kites released. The boom's dust circled above the sky until its sails were cinders.

SWALLOW ORBIT

Whenever Iris surfaces, the river cannot swim. Her worms mirror the surge of a squid ascending. Her waves are clotted with clouds. She salts the shore with an inch of her skin. Swallows orbit her steam.

FERAL DROSS

Minus's house moaned. The river maced his cocoon with moss. Feral dross. *This is the most cursed relief,* he spat. A cloud stooped down to boo.

BLACK BEACON

It is not seeking, like a child, the eyes of an animal. The infant and the animal have altered their instincts. They know that they do not know the darkness of trees. The house holds pollen. The house holds pollen and a tree beacons black. They know its not-body becomes what it surrounds. It surrounds what it is not seeking. It sleeps beside what the house keeps out.

FLOODED OUD

His palms become a hive for snow. He feeds them blisters. He skims. Old beasts eat the salt from his hands. He lets them crowd his sum.

SISTER SEQUENCE

No longer fur-covered, Iris begins blindfolded. One hand flails to map the atmosphere. Her cinema is a camera on two small children. This is the story of two films of a horse in the career of a woman lost in the woods. Might the river's description trace her tide? How does a sister sequence her streets?

DEER TONGUE

Minus converges his lambs with an asp. He coats the candles with sugar and waits. *Whenever I pick up her voice,* he writes, *I hover above my letters. I steep in the trees, unsigned.*

IRIS'S SALIVA

Iron filings filled my tongue. Then the sun found me.

COMMON CLOUD

I have been a patient tincture. A sifter, a watcher of snow. She thought her name would be stunned and it was. It was Iris Versus The Blur. It hurt to see the same snow twice. I was magnets or Minus or glass. I think we are being minted again. I think we are cotton or bread. There is always a different cost. A different cloth. A second coat. It takes some time in the positive press. We practiced our transfers today. Iris's insects were bluing the sky. *Hello. Helio threads.* She likes to call them dowsing crowds. I trace. I see parallel rays.

ACKNOWLEDGMENTS

Thanks to the editors of the following magazines: *Bayou, Caketrain, Coconut, Dear Navigator, Elective Affinities, Fascicle, Front Porch, Octopus, The Offending Adam, Omnidawn Blog, Hambone, Invisible Ear, The Ixnay Reader, Little Red Leaves, Parcel, Poets.org, Saltgrass, Skein,* and *Wildlife.* Portions of this work were published in the chapbooks *Negative Noon* (Minutes Books) and *Bee-Stung Aviary* (Further Adventures) and on a broadside printed by Brave Man Press.

Special thanks to Bin Ramke, Eleni Sikelianos, Selah Saterstrom, Jena Osman, Rachel Blau DuPlessis, Bhanu Kapil, Ryan Eckes, George Kalamaras, Stephanie G'Schwind, and Cole Swensen.